spiritual realities

Volume 3

ESCAPING DUALISM
Second Edition

Harold R. Eberle

WORLDCAST PUBLISHING
YAKIMA, WASHINGTON

Spiritual Realities, Volume III:
Escaping Dualism

© 2003 by Harold R. Eberle
First Edition, First Printing, 1997
Second Edition, First Printing 2003

Worldcast Publishing
P.O. Box 10653
Yakima, WA 98909-1653
(509) 248-5837
www.worldcastpublishing.com
office@worldcastpublishing.com

ISBN 1-882523-23-7
Cover by Jeff Boettcher

Unless otherwise stated, all biblical quotations are taken from the *New American Standard Bible* © 1977, The Lockman Foundation, La Habra, California 90631.

Printed in the United States of America

Credits and Thanks

This book would not have been possible if it had not been for Pastor James Leuschen of Spokane, WA, who helped me think through the many doctrinal issues and challenged me on numerous points. His theological insight brought me back down to Earth and forced me to communicate spiritual principles in understandable terms.

Also, I had input and editing advice from R.E. McMaster, Martha Brookhart, Peter Eisenmann, John Frady, Jane Johnson, and Dennis Jacobson. James Bryson and Annette Bradley deserve special mention for their expertise in the area of editing. Each of these has left his/her mark on these pages and on my life.

Table of Contents

Introduction

In Volumes I and II, I present foundational principles concerning the nature of humanity and how we can relate to the spiritual world. Before we go on to learn spiritual dynamics and discuss supernatural phenomena in later volumes, we must develop the truths in this volume.

In the following pages, we will uproot some false teachings concerning the nature of humanity. All Christians today, whether or not they realize it, have been influenced by these crippling doctrines. When they see the truth, their eyes are opened and they realize why they have not been experiencing the freedom that God promised. As we expose these false teachings, I hope to show you a more biblical view of humanity, one that helps Christians live more successfully in this world, using the authority and provisions of God.

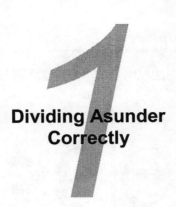

Dividing Asunder Correctly

Let's jump right into exposing a false teaching common in some Christian circles today. The issue here pertains to the nature of humanity. You may or may not be familiar with the following doctrine, however, all of Christianity has been influenced by it to some degree.

This doctrinal error begins with a misinterpretation of Hebrews 4:12. The King James Version of the Bible states this verse as follows:

> *For the word of God is quick, and powerful, and sharper than any twoedged sword, piercing even to the dividing asunder of soul and spirit, and of the joints and marrow, and is a discerner of the thoughts and intents of the heart.*

From this verse a teaching is sometimes brought forth which shows the sword (which is the Word of God) being dropped between the soul and the spirit of a person, dividing these two parts of a person's being one from the other.

MISUNDERSTANDING OF HEBREWS 4:12

This is a "dualistic" mindset. The word *dualistic* simply means "two-sided" or "two-fold."

Dualism may sound reasonable to many of my readers at this point, but I hope you will follow with me to see how subtly destructive this way of thinking becomes. Many Christians today have been indoctrinated completely into this philosophy, while others have been pulled in gradually without considering the implications. Some have been taught dualistic perspectives, even though Hebrews 4:12 never was used as the specific Scripture to promote it. To whatever extent a person has embraced dualistic patterns of thought, I want you to see some of the negative results in people's lives. But first I must show you how it has no basis in Scripture.

To cut at the very heart of this false doctrine, we need to see what the original manuscripts of the New Testament, which were written in the Greek language, literally say in Hebrews 4:12. Where we are told that the Word of God pierces even unto the dividing asunder of soul and spirit, the Greek word for "spirit" here is *pneumatos*. The first half of this word, *pneuma*, means *spirit*. The ending on this Greek word is, *atos*, which indicates possession. The word *pneumatos* therefore, is not to be translated *spirit*, but rather *of the spirit*.

This small distinction, which was overlooked by the translators of the King James Bible and a few other versions, has profound implications when we consider exactly how the Word of God divides. The correct interpretation of Hebrews 4:12 must indicate that the Word of God pierces even to the dividing asunder *of the soul* and *of the spirit*, of the joints and of the marrow. The passage does not say that the soul and spirit are divided one from another. It says that *both* of them are divided. The soul is divided and the spirit is divided.

In our diagram of a person's three-part nature, the sword must cut horizontally into a person, rather than vertically between the soul and spirit. The Greek literally tells us in Hebrews 4:12, that the Word of God pierces even to the depth of souls and to the depth of spirits in such a way that they themselves are divided.

CORRECT UNDERSTANDING OF HEBREWS 4:12

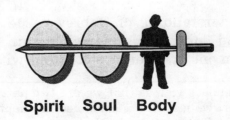

Spirit   Soul   Body

5

Any serious study in the original Greek Bible will confirm this. Let me quote from the Greek New Testament scholar Wuest in his *Word Studies in the Greek New Testament*:

> Piercing is the translation of "diikneomai" which means "to go through". The words "the dividing asunder of soul and spirit" do not mean, "the dividing asunder of the soul from spirit". Nor is it "the dividing asunder of the joints from the marrow". The case in Greek is the genitive of description, defining the action in the verb in this case. It is a going through the soul, a going through the spirit.

Wuest is a dichotomist* in his thinking; however, it is critical that we take note as to what the Bible actually says in Hebrews 4:12. Although the Greek Bible is clear concerning this, some Christian teachers today deny scholarly studies of the Greek language by continuing to teach that the soul should be divided from the spirit.

The understanding of Hebrews 4:12, which sees the soul and spirit being pierced within rather than divided from one another, is consistent with the rest of

---

* The dichotomist's view is that we are two-part beings rather than three-part beings. This is explained in Chapter One of Vol. II, entitled, *The Breath of God in Us*.

the Bible. The very next verse, Hebrews 4:13, goes on to tell us:

> *And there is no creature hidden*
> *from His sight, but all things are*
> *open and laid bare to the eyes of*
> *Him with whom we have to do.*

This verse gives us a contextual understanding of how God is able to see into the depths of a person's being, even into his or her spirit.

GOD SEES INTO THE DEPTHS OF ONE'S BEING

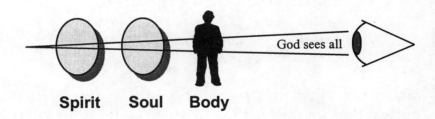

Spirit   Soul   Body

Similarly, in other passages we are told that the Word of God "pierces into," rather than separates the soul from the spirit. For example, when Peter preached on Pentecost Day, we are told that the word "pierced to the heart" (Acts 2:37). The Word of God has to penetrate into the spirit of the non-Christian; otherwise, the seed never could be planted within and salvation would be impossible. Even in the Christian's life there must be an ongoing planting of the Word of God within the spirit and soul. We must, therefore, think of the sword of God going into the person rather than dividing him or her in half. Nowhere in the Bible is there any passage which indicates that the soul and the spirit should be divided one from the other.

Why is this so important? In the following chapters I will show you implications that dramatically shift the way Christians live.

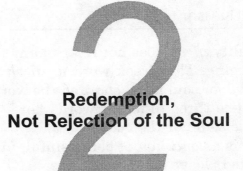

2
Redemption,
Not Rejection of the Soul

When Christians wrongly drop a sword between the spirit and the soul, dividing them one from another, they tend to think of the spirit as good, while thinking negatively about the soul and body. This dualistic way of thinking leads to several errors.

DUALISTIC THOUGHT

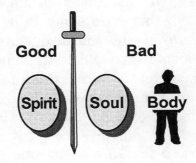

Good   Bad

Spirit   Soul   Body

The first error is in misunderstanding what the *flesh* is. Since dualists think of the soul and/or body as bad, they automatically equate the soul and/or body with the flesh. Or they try to identify some portion buried in the midst of the soul and body as flesh. Because of their dualistic mindset they have to locate the flesh somewhere within the soul and/or body.

In reality, *flesh* does not refer to any one part of a person's being. The Greek word for *flesh* is *sarx*. The Greek word for soul is *psuche,* and the word for body is *soma*. Notice three different words here. The flesh is neither the soul nor the body.

Flesh is a *condition* of being sinful, unregenerate, unsanctified. Jesus explained:

> *"That which is born of the flesh is flesh, and that which is born of the Spirit is spirit."*   (John 3:6)

With this definition, Jesus gave new meaning to the word *flesh*.

The term always had been used in a very natural sense to refer to the meat tissue of animals and people. Indeed, there are some Bible verses that use the term *flesh* in this natural sense; for example, when the priests in the Old Testament would offer the *flesh* of animals on the altar. Even in the New Testament there are some passages which use *sarx* to refer to the physical body (i.e., Acts 2:31; Gal. 4:13-14; Heb. 9:10).

However, in the New Testament there are many passages which contrast the word *flesh* with *spirit*. In those places the writers are using *sarx* to refer to the sinful nature of man. Jesus said that whatever is born of flesh is flesh and whatever is born of Spirit is spirit (John 3:6). By this we understand that whatever originates from a person's sinful nature is fleshly and is corrupted by sin. Whatever the Holy Spirit inspires and empowers is called *spirit*.

God ———> gives birth to ———> "spirit"

Sinful nature——> gives birth to ——> "flesh"

Paul used our Lord's definitions in First Corinthians when he told the Christians there that they were "men of flesh" (3:1), or "fleshly" (3:3). Paul pointed out that they were carnal, since they were fighting with one another and acting childish. Such characteristics are the deeds of the flesh (Gal. 5:19-21). In this context, the word *fleshly* can be interchanged with the term *carnal*.

What then is the flesh in relationship to a person's three-part being? It is not the soul. It is not the body. It is not a combination of the two, either. Rather **the flesh is whatever is in a person that has not yet been sanctified by God's Spirit.** If a person's behavior is evil, then those actions are corrupted, originating from the evil nature. Or in other words, "of the flesh." If a person has evil thoughts, then those thoughts are fleshly. If a person has desires contrary to the nature of God, then those desires have not been born of the Spirit. Whatever in a person's being has been produced by the sinful nature, that is flesh.

Flesh Is Whatever Is Born of the Carnal Nature

Fleshly Thoughts   **Fleshly Desires**

Fleshly Ideas   **Fleshly Habits**

As the Holy Spirit fills a Christian, the fleshly thoughts and desires are changed into holy thoughts and desires. Flesh is eliminated. The Holy Spirit transforms a person's being so that any and every part can be changed from fleshly to spiritual. Paul wrote in Romans 8:9:

> *However, you are not in the flesh*
> *but in the Spirit, if indeed the*
> *Spirit of God dwells in you.*

Notice how Paul said we actually can be free of the flesh. If the Holy Spirit truly was filling and giving birth to every thought and desire within our beings, then the flesh no longer would be resident within us. Everything within our beings then would be born of Him. The condition of being carnal no longer would exist in us.

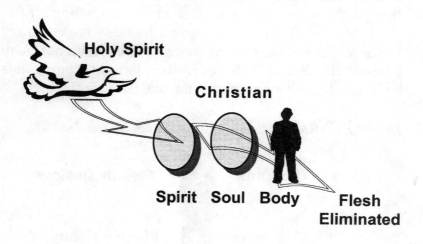

Holy Spirit

Christian

Spirit Soul Body   Flesh
                         Eliminated

This understanding is critical when we teach on how to live the victorious Christian life. Since the dualist thinks of the soul as evil, he or she always wants to subdue, subject, crucify, or control it. In contrast, the Christian who understands the Bible aims at redeeming the soul. The goal is to release the Holy Spirit from within so that one's fleshly desires and carnal thoughts will be expelled by God's nature. The evil deeds of the flesh can be put to death "by the Spirit" (Rom. 8:13). Two entirely different ways of living are produced.

The dualist never is able to enter fully into the grace and victory of our Lord Jesus. What we see in the life of dualistic Christians today is a tendency to battle with their flesh throughout their lives, never being able to conquer sins. This results from their belief that the flesh is forever resident within them and is a part of their unchangeable makeup.

Furthermore, once the dualist labels the soul and/ or body as evil, more rebellion is produced. It is impossible to accept such a negative way of thinking about a part of our beings without releasing condemnation upon ourselves. In Romans 7, Paul explained how the inner person wants to please God, but the outer person rebels. The more laws and condemnation placed upon the outer person, the more the rebellion to God's will grows, making the desires and thoughts within the soul evil and turning the body into a fleshly body of death. Therefore, as the dualist tries to control the outer person, rebellion increases. A war is established within the Christian with such a mindset. He or she ends up living as if there were two different people within. What is sad is that in the life of the true dualist, his or her doctrine demands that the outer person be kept under condemnation and laws. In fact, he or she will talk much about controlling the soul and crucifying the bodily desires. As a consequence, there is no escape from living with an internal war. This is a self-perpetuating war, and it only can escalate as more laws and condemnation are placed upon the soul and body.

DUALIST'S WAY OF LIVING

Laws/Condemnation/Control

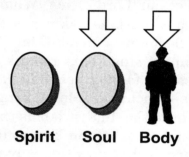

Spirit   Soul   Body

In Romans 8, Paul went on to explain how the Christian can break the cycle of war and bring the outer person to life, just as the inner person is alive. Paul taught how the outer person is made alive unto God as the believer escapes from condemnation and legalism (Rom. 8:1-3), and then releases the flow of the Spirit from within (Rom. 8:4-11). As a consequence, the soul and the body of the Christian are made alive by the Holy Spirit, which means that the desires originating within each will be made holy and according to God's will. The soul and the body literally are sanctified so that the thoughts and desires of the whole person become holy. No longer is a war necessary between the inner person and the outer person.*

The good news is that we can be sanctified entirely—spirit, soul, and body. This was Paul's prayer for the early Christians:

> *Now may the God of peace Himself sanctify you entirely; and may your spirit and soul and body be preserved complete, without blame at the coming of our Lord Jesus Christ.* (I Thess. 5:23)

Understanding this, we can see that we do not want any separation between the soul and the spirit. In fact, our aim must be for the opposite. Victorious living requires a complete and total union of the spirit and the soul so that the life within the spirit is entirely permeating the soul. In the same way, we want everything within our spirits emanating outward to flood our bodies so that they, too, will be transformed by the nature of God within.

The role of the Word of God in the ongoing Christian walk is not to be separating the spirit from the soul. It is the Word of God which is able to pierce into our beings, removing anything that is not in line with the nature of God. We must see the Word as piercing us in *shish kebab* fashion. As we allow the Word of God to come into us, it penetrates our entire beings.

---

* For further teaching on the victorious Christian life from this perspective, read the author's book, *Grace, the Power to Reign.*

We, therefore, must long for the pure milk of the Word, that by it we may grow in respect to salvation (I Peter 2:2). As we renew our minds and submit to the anointed ministry of God's Word, our spirits, souls, and bodies are brought into agreement in a progressive manner as we are transformed into His image, from glory to glory.

THE WORD OF GOD PIERCES IN SHISH KEBAB FASHION

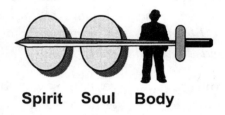

Spirit   Soul   Body

Please notice the difference between this way of living and the dualistic approach. The dualist is trying to conquer the desires of his or her soul and body, while the Christian should be trying to make the soul and body alive by the power of the Holy Spirit. Of course, a Christian should not yield to desires not yet sanctified. The proper biblical view of how we are to walk the victorious Christian life is one of releasing the flow of the rivers of life from within. This produces an entirely different way of living. This way of living works.

Knowing God's Will

In my own ministry I travel and speak to thousands of Christians in various denominations and groups. It is easy to see from this perspective how certain doctrines influence people on a large scale. When Christians are shown the truth in these areas, their eyes open to see things in an entirely new light.

A major area of confusion in the life of the dualistic Christian pertains to knowing God's will. Because the dualist thinks of the soul and body as evil, and the spirit as good, he/she wrongly concludes that God only leads through a person's spirit. At the same time, the dualist tries to deny the soul and body, thinking that all desires arising from within them are fleshly or from the devil.

DUALIST'S THINKING

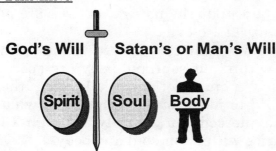

God's Will | Satan's or Man's Will

Spirit | Soul | Body

There is some truth to recognizing how God's will can be made known through the spirit of a person. The Bible tells us:

> *The spirit of man is the lamp of the LORD....*   (Prov. 20:27)

God communicates with people through their spirits.

However, what comes out of the soul and body of a person is not automatically evil.

Consider a mother who desires to care for her children. This is a very natural desire. It is God-instilled by creation. A woman does not have to be a Christian to have the related desires. God wants her to yield to those natural, motherly instincts.

Think of the physical desires to eat. These are not evil. Of course, these desires can be corrupted, but God placed hunger within people to motivate them to survive.

We also can talk about the natural desires for sexual relations. The normal physical passions that a husband and wife have for each other are good (I Tim. 4:3-4). In Romans 1:26-27, we can read about evil people who abandon the natural, marital desires and begin to lust after homosexual relationships. We are shown there that the natural desires are good, while the unnatural are evil.

What we want to see here is that some natural desires within our soul and body are good, and some are bad. We must not reject all, but rather discern. Our sword to judge what is right and what is wrong must be pierced horizontally through the desires which arise within our soul and body.

CORRECTLY DIVIDING

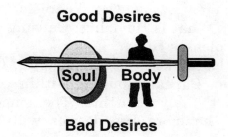

The same can be said for our thoughts and emotions. We should not think of all of them as our enemies. On the contrary, the ability to think is God-given. We were created with emotions to stir us to action and help us succeed in life. God does not want us to deny these aspects of our nature, but rather to discern and yield to those which are good.

The mother who feels love for her children is having emotions in line with God's will. The father who has thoughts on how to provide for his loved ones will be doing God's will by continuing to think and plan along those lines. Of course, fleshly thoughts and emotions can arise within us. However, our main point here is that God works through our nature.

This truth is even more profound when we consider the leading of God in the life of the Christian. Philippians 2:13 tells us:

> *...for it is God who is at work in you, both to will and to work for His good pleasure.*

The promises in the Old Testament assure us that God will put His Spirit in us and "cause us to walk in His ways" (i.e., Ez. 36:27). Where is God working? Within you. What is He doing? Causing you to desire to do what pleases Him.

As we learned in the last chapter, God is transforming you. Carnal thoughts within you are being replaced with holy thoughts. The longer you walk with God, the more His desires will become your desires.

God's will, then, is not something outside of ourselves. Dualistic thinking tends to see God's will as some mysterious voice floating in the spiritual realm. It is common to hear dualists say things, such as:

> "I want God's will, not my will."
> "I want God's thoughts, not my thoughts."
> "I do not want to act out of my emotions, but by
> the leading of the Holy Spirit."

Such statements are based on a misunderstanding of how God leads His children. Notice they assume that the person's will, thoughts, and emotions are contrary to God's will, thoughts, and emotions. That way of thinking is wrong.

Of course, Jesus prayed in the Garden of Gethsemane that the Father's will be done and not His own will (Luke 22:42). Indeed, *there can be times* when the human will must be conquered and brought into submission to the will of God. But that is not the norm nor standard. We should not live our daily lives trying to conquer all of our desires.

God makes His will known primarily in and through the life of the believer. Do you want to know what God's desire is for a certain situation? Ask God's people what their desires are for that situation. For example, most Christians want for their cities peace, love, revival, young people walking with God, and the salvation of souls. That is also what God wants. The two are not in conflict with each other, but the same.

Dualists often ask, "How do I know if it is the Holy Spirit leading me or my own emotions?" Notice, they already have separated in their minds the Spirit's leading from their own emotions. Unfortunate mistake!

What we must do is rotate the sword and ask the question, "Are these emotions according to God's will?" If they are, then the Christian will be doing God's will by yielding to those emotions. When Christians yield to the emotions stirred by God, they are yielding to the Holy Spirit. It is wrong, therefore, to try to separate one's emotions from God's leading.

Similarly, one's thoughts are the avenues through which God leads. Dualistic Christians do not understand this. In their confusion, they will try to separate their own thoughts from God's thoughts. They see the two as opposing each other and constantly at war. The truth is that when Christians are filled with the Holy Spirit, then their thoughts are God's thoughts. The Holy Spirit flows within the believers' innermost being, rising within their minds and revealing the thoughts of God. Christians then have the mind of Christ made manifest in their minds (I Cor. 2:16).

The way to be led by the Holy Spirit in one's daily

life is simply to yield to the Holy Spirit, not to try to subdue one's own thoughts. God's thoughts then become the individual's thoughts, and to follow one's own thoughts is to follow the Holy Spirit.

This is not to give credence to fleshly habits, desires, or thoughts. I am not throwing out discernment. I simply am pointing out that God is in the process of revealing His will to us by conforming our nature to His.

How, then, can a Christian know the will of God for his or her own life? By looking at the desires and thoughts within his or her own being. Do you want to know what God wants you to do in life? Then ask yourself, "What do I want to do in life?" This includes both naturally-oriented desires and those related to more spiritual issues.

A mother who has desires to spend time with her children is doing God's will by spending time with her children. God's will is not contrary to her will. It is, in fact, the same. The man who wants to provide financially for his family is doing God's will by doing what he wants to do. Even in the spiritual areas this is true. The believer who desires to pray is doing God's will by praying. The one who passionately desires to go overseas and preach the gospel as a missionary is being obedient to God by doing what he or she most wants to do.

Again, let me say, I am not giving credence to every evil lust and thought one has. We must drop the sword within our own beings and separate the carnal from the good. However, that sword is dropped within our own beings. The good thoughts and desires of God are not outside of us. They are there, arising within our own minds, hearts, and entire beings.

I could talk here about the many other ways that God leads us, such as through the Bible, through other people, through circumstances, etc. God also communicates with people, giving spiritual impressions, dreams, and visions. I have much to say about all that in coming volumes. But here I am settling foundational issues first. Our main point is that God is in each of us, in one's whole being—body, soul, and spirit. Dualists never fully embrace that truth.

What makes it even more difficult for dualists to know God's will is the tendency to think of spiritual things as good and the natural as evil. Dualists not only divide the spirit from the soul/body, but they tend to divide the entire spiritual realm from the natural. In their thinking they have dropped a sword which separates the two worlds.

DUALIST'S THINKING

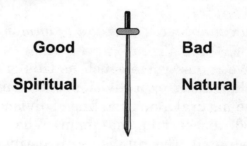

Good	Bad
Spiritual	Natural

This way of thinking tends to make people feel as if they are doing God's will only while they are engaged in spiritual activities. For example, the mother who has to care for little children may feel condemned because she is not praying all the time. The man who works 40 to 60 hours a week may feel inferior to the one who sits at home trying to tap into the spirit. Sometimes an entire church congregation will have embraced this dualistic mindset, and whenever anyone engages in naturally-oriented labors, they are made to feel as if they are failing God and are out of His will.

Here is an eye-opening truth on which every dualist needs to meditate: Jesus was no less in the will of the Father as a carpenter than He was during the last three years of His ministry. If this thought shakes you, then you have dualistic thinking.

In making their division between the spiritual world and the natural, dualists often misinterpret several key Bible passages. There is a *line* in their field of vision that divides everything in half, and often that division line falls in the wrong place.

For example, dualists commonly misinterpret Matthew 6:24, where we are told:

You cannot serve God and mammon.

Dualists love to use verses such as this one, because they can align their own division between the spiritual and the natural along the line of division between serving God and serving mammon. When these two lines are equated, the dualist can justify not doing anything naturally oriented because, after all, it would be "serving mammon." Working a job is contrasted with serving God. Cleaning the house is equated with being a slave to natural things. Taking care of possessions is the same as seeking natural things, rather than the kingdom of God.

DUALISTIC DECEPTION

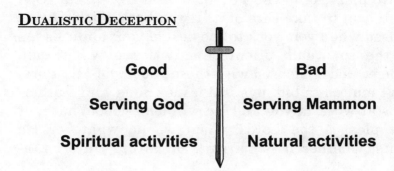

Good	Bad
Serving God	Serving Mammon
Spiritual activities	Natural activities

In reality, serving God may mean working 40 to 60 hours a week. Serving mammon is disobeying God's plan for one's life. Pleasing God has absolutely nothing to do with the line between the spiritual and the natural worlds. What must be done is to rotate the dualist's sword by 90 degrees.

BIBLICAL TRUTH:

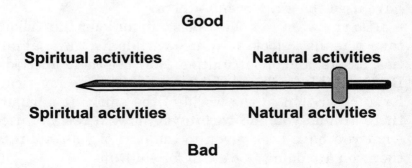

Good

Spiritual activities   Natural activities

Spiritual activities   Natural activities

Bad

How do you know God's will? Don't think in terms of spiritual versus natural. Some natural things you do are pleasing to the Father. If you have a car, God wants you to take care of it. If you have a job, God is pleased when you work to the best of your abilities. As for the spiritually-oriented activities in which you engage, God is pleased with those you do for His glory. Don't make it a big mystical issue. He is your Father. He is at work in you and He will lead you. What is it that pleases the Lord? When we do whatever He wants, whether it is spiritual or natural in orientation.

When we talk about pleasing God, we ultimately must develop a picture from His throne of judgment.

Consider the parable Jesus told of the three men who received certain talents (Matt. 25:14-30). The two men who used their talents received great rewards, while the one who hid his talent was punished. Of course, we know that every person will be judged, first and foremost, on his acceptance or rejection of Jesus Christ. However, beyond that, there will be different rewards given to believers, depending upon how they have used the gifts given to them.

Do you want to know God's will for your life? Then take a realistic look at your own talents, gifts, abilities, assets, and opportunities. Now use them for God. Do not think God's will for your life is some mystical formula written in the world of the spirit. It is right there around you and within you now. When you use what you have been given to the best of your ability, then you are doing God's will for your life.

Dualists judge themselves and others wrongly.

They examine how successful people have been at denying their own desires and detaching from the natural world. Those who are extreme dualists either consciously or subconsciously feel best about themselves when they are doing something which either they do not like to do and/or when they are unsuccessful in natural affairs. This may sound strange, but it is common to find a person who fully has embraced dualistic thinking to be financially hurting, owning nothing of value, not involved in anything significant in society, and suffering rejection by other people. I even have known some dualistic people who have gone through a divorce, and who view it as a "price they had to pay." Of course, most dualists do not show their errors so obviously, but they manifest in underlying feelings and beliefs throughout their own persons and experiences.

In contrast, Christians who have the proper biblical view evaluate their own lives on the basis of fruit. They look at their own lives and see how successful they have been in walking out their Christian beliefs. For them the vital questions are, "Is our Christianity actually working in our marriages, in our homes, and with our children? Are we successful at paying our bills and blessing others? Are our lives impacting and changing society in some substantial way?" Healthy Christians have a realistic view of their lives, in which they honestly look to see what tangible results are coming forth from their labors. Positive results are the proof of their faith.

These principles are key. In Volumes IV and V we will spend more time looking at issues concerning the spiritual dimension and how to discern the supernatural. Before we can do that, your "feet need to be on the ground." Talking about spiritual issues can send people into a whole mystical lifestyle that misses what Christianity is all about. Dualists already have lost touch with reality. Don't fall for that deception.

Now let us look more carefully at the soul and its function in the ongoing daily life of the Christian. In developing this understanding, it will be helpful for us to draw a few more contrasts between the dualistic view and the biblical perspective. Our goal is to see when and how the soul is to be involved in our daily lives and in our relationships to the spiritual realm.

Serve God with Your Whole Soul

The dualistic mindset has produced many misconceptions concerning the value and function of the soul. Advocates over the years have coined certain words, such as "soulical" and "soulish." You may or may not be familiar with these terms, but you need to see that the deception in such words lies in placing the soul of a person in a negative context.

The basic commission from God to His people is:

> "...to serve the Lord your God
> with all your heart and with all
> your soul...."   (Deut. 10:12)

"All your soul" means "all your soul." Dualists have a difficult time with this. They would rather sentence the soul to death than see it resurrected to life. The true biblical ideal is that Christians are not living their fullest for God until "everything" in their souls is being used for God.

There are New Testament verses just as clear on this subject. For example, Ephesians 6:6 tells Christians that they should "be doing the will of God from the heart"; this last word *heart* is mistranslated from the Greek word, *psuche*. What we really are being told to do in this verse is to serve God from our soul.

Colossians 3:23 similarly exhorts us:

> *Whatever you do, do your work heartily, as for the Lord rather than for men....*

The word translated *heartily* in this verse is from the Greek words *ek psuche*, meaning, *from the soul*. It is clear that our labors should be performed with our entire soul involved.

Consider now what we would call natural talents and abilities, such as logical thinking, organizational skills, and planning. Dualists tend to associate these with the soul of a person, and therefore, consciously or subconsciously reject them. If they do not condemn outrightly the associated abilities, they tend to view them as "lower functions of life," in contrast to the more "spiritually-oriented" activities. Upon the natural abilities of a person the dualists would apply their negative label, "soulish."

Let me give you an example of how dualists may misjudge a specific situation based on their rejection of the soul. If we were to talk about some well-known minister used by God to evangelize thousands of people, Christians generally would be supportive. If that minister were to speak in a stadium and huge crowds gathered to hear the Word of God, we probably would rejoice to hear of the event. Even greater would be the rejoicing if God performed healings and miracles through the minister. When we watch the event on television, we would see the minister preaching under the anointing of God, and Christians everywhere would be happy to be on the same team.

Now if we discuss how much work went into such an event, some people's views may change. Instead of focusing on the single minister being used by God, let's note how many ushers are there keeping the crowd orderly. Then let's talk about the custodians who clean the toilets and the stadium afterward. And how about the financial experts who budget, plan, and organize? Then there are the advertising experts, artists, sound people, lighting crew, engineers, parking lot attendants, etc. Managing each area is an administrator using all of his or her planning and organizational skills. Hundreds of people are working together, even though the viewers' eyes all will be focused on the single preacher standing on the platform.

Dualists like to recognize the anointing upon the leader, and they may give credit also to the prayer warriors behind the scenes; but they would hesitate in admitting that the administrators, advertisers, engineers, financial managers, etc., are equally as important. If they are considered important, it will be with a subconscious attitude that all those "natural gifts and talents" are necessary burdens. The naturally-oriented activities never are valued as highly as the spiritual.

In contrast, the Christian with a healthy, biblical view sees the financial administration and the planning board just as glorifying to God and essential as the minister up front. The spiritual activities are no more pleasing to God than the natural. That which is associated with the soul is not of lesser value than what some would label as "belonging to the spirit."

I already have discussed the role of emotions and thoughts. Of course, people can be darkened in their understanding, and their emotions may be fleshly. However, the concept of humanity that we are developing here is that *all of one's being* can be sanctified and used for God's glory.

The soul and the body offer us the means by which we are to "walk out" our Christian lives. "Whole Christians" may obtain authority from God and inspiration through the spirit, but they use their minds, emotions, organizational skills, and everything else within their ability in order to walk out God's plan for their lives. They serve God with their *whole souls* and with *all of their strength*. This is the commandment of God.

BIBLICAL UNDERSTANDING

Inspiration & Authority — Walk out in the natural

Spirit Soul Body

We will speak more clearly on this "whole lifestyle" later, but here we need to correct one more dualistic misconception concerning the soul. In talking about relationships, dualists condemn what they call "soul ties." This term is used to refer to the bonding between two individual's souls. The dualist almost always uses this term in the negative sense (because, again, dualists see the soul as evil), and Christians, therefore, are exhorted to break all soul ties between themselves and others.

In contrast, several Bible passages talk in a positive way about the people of God becoming of one heart and one soul (i.e., Acts 4:32). The Apostle Paul talked about Timothy who was "of kindred soul" to him (Phil. 2:20; original Greek: *isopsuchos*). Paul specifically told *all Christians* that they should endeavor to be "one in soul" (Phil. 2:2; original Greek: *sum psuchoi*). In First Samuel 18:1, we are told that the "soul of Jonathan was knit to the soul of David...." Each of these bondings involving people's souls is spoken of as good.

Of course, not every relationship between people is according to God's will. I am challenging the dualistic mentality that categorically rejects anything pertaining to the soul. Christians must, by an act of their wills, choose with whom they will be bonded. We must discern which relationships are of God. Soul ties, according to His direction, are good.

PROPER DISCERNMENT OF SOUL TIES

Good
Soul Ties

Soul Ties
Bad

I have been talking about the implications of wrongly dividing the soul from the spirit. And although I am discussing these implications, do not lose sight of my beginning discussion, where I showed that the foundational thinking of dividing the soul from the spirit originated from a mistranslation of Hebrews 4:12. The entire concept of dropping a sword between the two is contrary to what the Bible really teaches. I am spending all this time unraveling a confused mass of teachings, all stemming from a mistranslation and misinterpretation of one verse in the Bible.

Different Christian groups have been influenced in varying degrees by dualistic thought. Perhaps the strongest dualistic teacher during the Twentieth Century was a man named Watchman Nee. Watchman Nee was an amazing Christian leader, greatly used to establish the home church movement in China. He paid a high price for his Christian stand in a country then antagonistic toward the gospel. However, he was also dualistic in his theology, and he wrote several books promoting that way of thinking. Those books have influenced tens of thousands of Christians throughout the world.

To whatever degree Christians have embraced dualistic thinking, they will be helped by reconsidering the related issues. Let this one fact now be established: Christians should use their souls, and in fact, can only fulfill God's command by serving Him with all of their strength and with all of their souls.

Soul Power

In their confusion, dualists condemn what they call "soul power." When a dualist is talking about soul power, he or she is referring to a variety of characteristics including—but not limited to—personal charisma, confidence, a strong sense of identity, and the forces which flow out of these attributes to influence other people. Strict dualists condemn all such soul power as evil.

At the same time, dualists claim that all energy coming forth from the spirit of the Christian is good. Realize that the only reason they call soul power evil is because they already have decided doctrinally that the soul is evil. They wrongly have dropped a sword between the spirit and the soul, and sentenced everything in the soul to their negative judgment.

DUALISTIC DECEPTION CONCERNING DISCERNMENT

Good   Spirit power   Soul power   Bad

In order to sort out truth from error, let's begin by discussing *strength of soul*. Dualists tend to reject anything of the soul; and, therefore, they immediately have to conclude that strength of soul is bad.

Such thinking is wrong. King David, for example, praised God, saying:

> *Thou didst make me bold with strength in my soul.* (Ps. 138:3b)

Strength of soul here is a characteristic to be desired. King David was referring to his own level of confidence and leadership strength. God gave him strength of soul.

There are numerous other Bible passages talking about restoration, health, blessings, or prosperity of soul; for example:

> *The Lord is my shepherd...*
> *He restores my soul....*
>   (Ps. 23:1a, 3a)

> *But the soul of the diligent is made fat.*   (Prov. 13:4b)

> *Beloved, I pray that in all respects you may prosper and be in good health, just as your soul prospers.*   (III John vs. 2)

In Acts 14:22 we read how Paul went from one group of Christians to another, "strengthening the souls of the disciples." It is God's will for Christians to be strong of soul. It was John's prayer that they may prosper within their souls. When the Holy Spirit floods Christians, their souls are made vibrant and bold. This is a work of God in our lives. Strength and health of soul is *good*.

For a comparison I can talk about the strength and health of the human body. We know that each of us should serve God with all of our strength. It is a good thing when a man on the mission field uses his physical strength to reach people in remote regions with the gospel. Also, the lady using her strength to feed the poor in her city may be fulfilling God's calling on her life. The strength and health of the human body is a good thing which every Christian should be using for God's glory.

Dualists do not understand this fully. In reference to strength of the body or of the soul, they may say, "I want God's strength, not my strength!" A dualist tries to separate the two. That is foolish and wrong. For the Christian trying to serve God, his or her strength is God's strength. The two must not be separated. God may increase the strength of a person supernaturally, and God often does use weak people. However, we must not fall for the dualistic deception which sees one's own strength as evil, and, therefore, exults in being weak. The truth is that God rejoices in the strength of His people.

I have been trying to impact you with the fundamental truth that we should serve God with all of our strength. This includes not only our body; but the great commandment specifically tells us to serve Him with our entire soul. We now need to see that this includes *soul power* or any other energy that comes from the soul of the Christian.

In Volume II, I explained how the soul of a person is a created entity, limited in size and shape. The soul does not emanate out of the body, as the spirit may. In other words, it does not flow from out of the body in the form of energy.

The term *soul power* is, therefore, a misnomer, and that is why it is nowhere in the Bible. When the dualists talk about *soul power* or *soul energy,* they are confusing this with spiritual energy. The soul can and does act as a doorway for energy to flow from the spirit of the person, or from the spiritual world into the natural. However, even the idea that the soul flows out as energy is questionable. What actually happens is that spiritual energy can flow through the soul of a person.

SPIRITUAL ENERGY FLOWS THROUGH THE SOUL

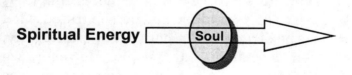

Spiritual Energy — Soul

Of course, some of the spiritual energy flowing *through* the soul can be evil. Therefore, the Christian must use discernment. That discernment is not the same as the dualist's trying to divide between the soul and spirit. Rather, we must look more deeply at the *spiritual energy* involved. The sword which divides must be rotated 90 degrees, separating both the entire person and the spiritual world. People have some power within their own being, and there may be evil elements within the soul of a person needing sanctification. But the real issue when talking about spiritual power is in discerning that which comes from God and that which comes from Satan.

DISCERNING SPIRITUAL ENERGY

Good Spiritual Energy

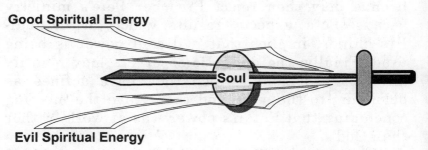

Evil Spiritual Energy

Notice how different this way of thinking is from the dualist's. The dualist tries to separate energy coming forth from the spirit of a person from energy coming forth from the soul. That is foolish. The biblical perspective looks to see if spiritual energy is flowing from God or from Satan. Whether or not the soul is involved is irrelevant.

Now, let's compare the discernment of a dualist with the discernment of a Christian with a biblical view. Consider a preacher who attracts crowds easily. This preacher I will call Pete. When Preacher Pete speaks, he is very dramatic, and the audience seems to become caught up in all that he is saying. If he has an altar call at the end of his meeting, many people usually respond. Pete has come to expect these results.

Dualists sitting in the midst of the congregation will tend to judge the preacher, either consciously or subconsciously, by trying to divide spirit from soul. They may be skeptical of Preacher Pete because he seems too emotional. Depending upon the skeptics' "type" of dualistic thinking, they may focus on how the audience seems to be mesmerized. Our dualistic friends may then reject Preacher Pete's ministry because Pete "expects" results, which, in the dualists' minds, implies that evil soul power is being used. Finally, the dualistic observers may identify any other elements which they have defined as belonging to the soul, and then leave the meeting concluding that Satan's power was at work, rather than God's.

In contrast, Christians with a more biblical understanding will evaluate Preacher Pete's ministry on an entirely different basis (Volume I, Chapter 12). They will listen to Pete's teaching to see if it agrees with the written Word of God. They will be sensitive to the spirit of the whole meeting to see if it glorifies Jesus Christ. And they will observe the fruit. If many people are being drawn to Jesus, and the teaching is according to the Word of God, then God's power is at work.

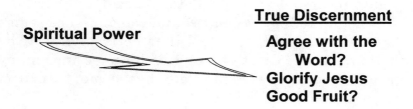

Spiritual Power

True Discernment

Agree with the Word?
Glorify Jesus
Good Fruit?

Allow me to repeat: The question of soul power versus spirit power is irrelevant. To think in those categories is deceptive and unbiblical. What is important is to discern between the Spirit of God and evil spirits.

This issue is important. Some ministers have become enslaved by a dualistic doctrine which has kept them from being effective. One well-known evangelist was used to lead thousands of people to God, but then a strict dualist pulled him aside and filled his mind with all kinds of false, unbiblical ideas about the soul being evil. This evangelist then became filled with doubts. He stopped his evangelistic work for fear that he might release this evil "soul power." When he did try preaching again, he battled to keep himself from showing any emotion or directing any energy toward those to whom he was speaking. As a result, he never again was used to bring people to Jesus in any significant way.

The preacher in the example I just gave you was Evan Roberts, who led the revival in the country of Wales. That revival was one of the most dramatic movings of God's power seen in any nation in history. After young Evan Roberts preached one evening, he was pulled aside by Jesse Penn-Lewis, who convinced him that he had been using soul power. After two years of some of the most effective preaching the world ever has seen, Roberts stopped his preaching ministry for fear that he might again use this "evil soul power." A short time later, he co-authored a book with Jesse Penn-Lewis in which he denied much of the very revival he had been used to stir. The book,

41

entitled *War On the Saints,* has been revised and reprinted several times. Although it contains some noteworthy warnings, the original printing condemned much of the revival from a dualistic perception.

In history we also find Jesse Penn-Lewis as the one who discipled Watchman Nee—of whose writings I already have warned you.

The example of Evan Roberts ending his preaching ministry may seem extreme, but I hope you see its implications within your own life. The Bible teaches us to do whatever we do "wholeheartedly"—that is, in Greek, *with all our soul* (Col. 3:23). Christians should not be bound with fears that evil soul power is resident within them. They need not hold back from showing emotions or releasing all that is within their souls. On the contrary, believers should direct their lives to serve God confidently with all of their souls and all of their strengths. Of course, evil may be released through a person, and we must be sensitive and able to discern this (as we will teach in the next chapter), but the question of soul power versus spirit power must <u>not</u> be the focus of our judgment.

One more area of application we can mention here is intercessions and prayers. Some Christians are afraid to put any energy or force behind their prayers because they do not want the "evil soul power" to be released. As a consequence, their prayers always are weak and without passion. To see the truth, all we need to do is consider our Lord praying in the Garden of Gethsemane; there He fell on His face and prayed with such fervency that His sweat became as drops of blood (Luke 22:44). At that time He also said to His disciples, "My soul is deeply grieved, to the point of death; remain here and keep watch with Me" (Matt. 26:38b). Effective prayer sometimes incorporates the entire being of a person, and attempts at subduing the soul are foolish.

To think and judge with a dualistic mindset is to look with blinded eyes. Years ago when I was in college, I had a roommate who was color-blind. Laundry day for him was a terrible ordeal, because he could not match his socks properly one to the other. Since he could not see the obvious color differences, he carefully would examine differences in size, texture, and amount of wear on each sock. Unfortunately, even with his most careful examinations, he still made some rather comical mistakes, wearing different colored socks at the same time. In a corresponding fashion, dualists tend to be "color-blind." Their minds are doctrinally trained to look for that which they associate with the soul, and to reject accordingly. Such a trained mindset leads to serious misjudgments. If people are programmed by their doctrine to look for certain natural aspects, they often will miss the obvious identification marks of God's work—marks which the Bible clearly teaches are the true bases by which to judge.

What I am asking you to do is to judge spiritual things on the basis of their agreement with the Word of God, their exaltation of Jesus Christ, and the fruit produced. This will open your eyes to see and free you to serve God with your whole heart, soul, and mind.

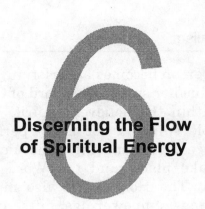

Discerning the Flow
of Spiritual Energy

I have explained the error of dualism in its attempt to divide the spirit from the soul. I have shown how dualists' negative view of the soul is wrong. Now let's turn our focus toward the spirit and the spiritual energy that can flow through a person. The dualist sees the Christian's spirit as good and incapable of error. This, we will see, is a serious mistake.

DUALIST'S THINKING

Good

Spirit &
Spiritual Energy
in the Christian

Dualists believe that the Christian's spirit has been made perfect through the born-again experience. In Volume II, Chapter 6, I explained why this "perfect-spirit doctrine" is contrary to what the Bible teaches. I will not repeat that whole discussion, but I will briefly mention the key points.

When a person becomes a Christian, God breathes new life into his/her spirit. The Word of God is planted as a seed within the believer's spirit. However, the person's whole spirit is not made perfect instantaneously. There is an ongoing sanctification process that must take place, and the Word will grow to produce fruit. The Holy Spirit also may give additional anointings, empowerings, gifts, and grace. For Scriptural references of these truths, I refer you back to Chapter 6 of Volume II.

The Christian's spirit also may be wounded, oppressed, broken, and/or defiled. This last characteristic is key and worth mentioning again. The Apostle Paul wrote concerning how a Christian's spirit can be "defiled."

> *Therefore, having these promises, beloved, let us cleanse ourselves from all defilement of flesh and spirit, perfecting holiness in the fear of God.* (II Cor. 7:1)

Notice that Paul is talking to Christians, "beloved," who have the promises of God. To brothers and sisters in Christ, Paul writes that they are to cleanse themselves from defilement of flesh *and spirit.*

So then, we see that the Christian's spirit is not perfect, but, indeed, can be defiled, broken, oppressed, etc. It also can be benefited through the ongoing work of the Holy Spirit.

It is just as important for us to see that evil spiritual substance can be brought into the life and being of a Christian.

Earlier (Volume II, Chapter 8) I explained how the heart is the pivotal point in a person's being. From the heart flow all the issues of life (Prov. 4:23), and into it flows spiritual energy. Just as the physical heart draws in blood and then forces it out throughout the entire body, so also the heart of the inner person receives and emanates spiritual life.

Both good and evil can be drawn within. The heart is as soil receiving the good things of God (Matt. 13:19-23). Evil, too, may be "conceived" within the heart. James wrote that when we lust for things, we actually conceive that evil within ourselves. In time, the evil conceived will grow as seeds to give birth to sin (James 1:14-15).

The "seeds" of the devil grow just as the seeds of God's kingdom. Our Lord Jesus explained this in a parable of an evil man sowing bad seeds in a field of good wheat (Matt. 13:24-30). Both the good seeds and the bad seeds came up simultaneously to produce their good and bad fruit, respectively.

Jesus also told us, "For the mouth speaks out of that which fills the heart" (Matt. 12:34). Since we have both good and evil within us, both good and evil will come forth at different times.

Consider George, a Christian man who loves God, and who was hurt emotionally in a church split. As George meditates on how unjustly he was treated, he draws within himself seeds of bitterness. Then one day George speaks out in a church service, and, at first, what he says seems very inspired by God, and everyone is greatly blessed. But then George makes a few comments that reveal the hurt in his heart, and bitterness actually pours out for a minute or two. Notice both good and evil coming out of George's mouth. We must discern between the two.

In James 3:9-11, we are told about the human tongue.

> *With it we bless our Lord and Father; and with it we curse men, who have been made in the likeness of God; from the same mouth come both blessing and cursing. My brethren, these things ought not to be this way. Does a fountain send out from the same opening both fresh and bitter water?*

The human being is compared with a fountain here and a contrast is made. The fountain does not release both good and evil at the same time, but a human being often does.

Sometimes that mixed flow is the result of a person's own bad heart motivations. Other times it is simply the result of the devil finding a foothold in the person's life. The devil is trying to deceive everyone, and at times we all submit to his temptations. At that moment we are allowing his evil nature to flow through us.

We can see this in several incidents in the Bible. For example, the disciples reacted wrongly when Jesus was rejected by a certain Samaritan village. In indignation they asked:

*"Lord, do You want us to com-
mand fire to come down from
heaven and consume them?"*
(Luke 9:54b)

Jesus responded, rebuking them and saying:

*"You do not know what kind of
spirit you are of...."* (Luke 9:55b)

The disciples, for a moment, were being motivated
and inspired by a spirit contrary to God's nature.

We can see a similar phenomenon in Peter's life.
In Matthew 16:13-16, Peter made the great declara-
tion of our Lord being the Son of God. Jesus responded
by telling Peter that the Father revealed, that is,
inspired this truth in him. But just six verses later,
we find Peter taking Jesus aside and trying to dis-
courage Him from His mission. Jesus responds by
saying to Peter, "Get behind Me, Satan!" (Matt.
16:23). We see, then, the first words Peter spoke were
inspired by God, and the second were inspired by the
devil.

We also can read in the Bible how other evil
spiritual influences came upon people. For example,
Isaiah rebuked the leadership of Egypt and declared
that God had sent a "spirit of distortion" upon them.

*The LORD has mixed within her
a spirit of distortion;
They have led Egypt astray in all
that it does,
As a drunken man staggers in
his vomit.* (Is. 19:14)

Notice that this deceiving spirit was "mixed" within them. As a consequence, some of the things they were inspired to do were right and some were wrong.

When there is a *mixed flow*, we still recognize the spiritual energy moving through a person. However, it is as if those rivers have become *polluted*.

A MIXED FLOW OF SPIRITUAL ENERGY

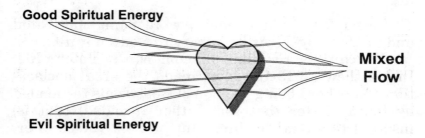

Good Spiritual Energy

Mixed Flow

Evil Spiritual Energy

Why is all this so important? I am showing you how evil spiritual influences can work through the Christian. This is important because it demands that we, therefore, judge the spiritual flow through every person.

The strict dualist will not allow judgment of the spiritual things he or she receives. Because they believe the Christian's spirit is good and perfect, they see no basis for even trying to discern that which flows out. Dualistic doctrine, in fact, forbids it.

Repeatedly in Church history, various groups have drifted into error because they did not allow any judgment of the spiritual things flowing through their leaders. In such groups, Christians were taught that the spirit is perfect, and, therefore, that no one should judge what comes forth through inspiration or revelation. Then, if deception creeps in, there is no defense, nor even the ability to discern. Anyone who disagrees with the leader is pushed aside. Even thoughts within the leader's mind that question his/her own activities are forcefully rejected. Sometimes the deceived leader will go so far as to say that everything he/she does while under the anointing is right from God's throne, and it must not be judged in any way. Then, if the leader gradually gets pushed away from biblical truth, strong deception takes over. The people involved continue to follow their leader without question because they have been trained never to judge his/her *"anointing."* Sooner or later, history repeats itself as destruction sweeps in and devastates the lives of those involved.

The Bible is very clear about us judging all spiritual impressions, revelations, manifestations, etc. The Apostle Paul gave instructions to the Corinthian believers.

> *When you assemble, each one has a psalm, has a teaching, has a revelation, has a tongue, has an interpretation.... And let two or three prophets speak, and let the others pass judgment.*
> (I Cor. 14:26b, 29)

Notice the clear instructions to judge that which comes forth by inspiration. Judgment only makes sense if, indeed, there is the possibility for error. Obviously, there is.

Hence, we see the need to drop the sword, as we are instructed, through the whole of a person's being, even unto the dividing asunder "of the spirit," that is, in Greek, *pneumatos*.

Allow me to give you a few examples from present-life situations.

Consider Carol, a Christian woman who is discipling a small group of new believers. She is doing an excellent work, as far as teaching the Word of God and making her students solid in their faith. However, in her heart there is also a hidden anger toward the whole church, and a bitterness because of problems which she experienced several years earlier. Although Carol tries not to let out the dark side of her feelings, it does come upon her listeners and actually is imparted into their lives. Soon her disciples are having similar thoughts and feelings of anger toward the church.

Not only bitterness, but other evil spiritual influences also can be transmitted from one person to another. Paul warned the Corinthian Christians about a sexually perverted man in their midst. He explained that if they allowed him to continue, the evil would spread to the rest of the church, just as leaven leavens a whole lump of dough (I Cor. 5:1-7).

I know of one minister who was traveling from church to church, teaching and praying for people. As he laid hands upon them and prayed, many received help and real healings in their bodies. However, some also began having various marriage problems immediately after their spiritual encounter. When this minister was investigated by some other Christian leaders, it was discovered that he had serious problems in his own marriage. He was transmitting, through the laying on of hands, not only healing power but also a destructive influence.

I dare say that every minister and every Christian has a "mixed flow." That is the very reason we are told to judge the spiritual gifts. Every time a certain preacher speaks before his congregation, he/she speaks from out of that which fills his/her heart. Hopefully, the minister is spiritually strong and in close communion with God; but within the heart of every person there remains open doors for the devil to find access. Until we have been completely sanctified—body, soul, and spirit—as Paul prayed (I Thess. 5:23), there remains the possibility for error and the necessity, therefore, for discernment.

The Christian must not be deceived. Even the most powerful leaders can have a mixed flow. King Saul, we are told, led the nation of Israel by the anointing of God (I Sam. 10:6-7). But then later in his life his heart became corrupted, and an evil spirit started to work upon and through him (I Sam. 16:14). We must not be overwhelmed by the anointing upon any man or woman, to the degree that we abandon discernment.

The sword must fall not only across the words, actions, and soul of a person, but also through his or her spirit. The spiritual impressions, revelations, and inspirations all must be judged (I Thess. 5:21).

7

Dualism: Seedbed
for Sexual Perversions

In addition to the problems already discussed, dualism is a seedbed for sexual perversions.

As I explain this, we must expand our thinking of dualistic thought. It is not limited to small Christian circles which misinterpret Hebrews 4:12. To some extent dualism has influenced our entire Western culture. It was the ancient Greek philosophers who spoke strongly in terms of dividing the spiritual world from the natural. Most prominently Plato (c. 427-347 BC) taught that only the spiritual things are significant and good; whatever is done in the natural, he said, is insignificant. This ancient Greek way of thinking is at the foundation of our Western society today. It has influenced the Church and the entire Western world.

GREEK WAY OF THINKING

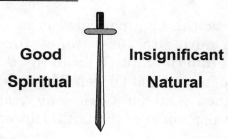

| Good | Insignificant |
| Spiritual | Natural |

The Greek philosopher, Plato, took the division made between the spiritual and natural realms, and applied it to the nature of humanity. He viewed the invisible, spiritual side of a person as the true person. He thought of the body as an insignificant, temporary container. This dualistic concept of humanity permeated the Greek culture.

GREEK VIEW OF MAN:

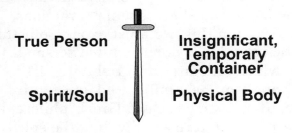

True Person		Insignificant, Temporary Container
Spirit/Soul		Physical Body

The logical conclusions of this philosophy led the Greeks into many problems, including sexual perversions. Because the spirit/soul was considered the real person, the physical body was completely separated with regard to moral responsibility. Therefore, many Greek philosophers taught that in the physical realm all forms of sexual perversion could be practiced, and that any participants still could be good and spiritually pure.

Dualistic thinking pervaded most of the intellectual world during the first two centuries. It became introduced into the Church primarily through leaders such as Augustine and Origen. These two men accomplished much good for Christianity, and they were each great defenders of the faith. However, they were both dualistic in their thinking, and hence, helped introduce the related thought patterns into theology.

Augustine was perhaps the most influential along these lines. He lived from 354 AD to 430 AD, during the time when the Roman government was embracing Christianity as its primary religion. Because the Roman government was at the height of its power, what the Emperor decreed on spiritual matters influenced the entire kingdom. Augustine was the most prominent theologian of the day, and hence, he was able to spread his understanding quickly and effectively throughout the known world.

Before becoming a Christian, Augustine was a student of Greek philosophy. Being trained in a strong dualistic environment and continuing to deal with the intellectual world of his day, he kept the spiritual world separate from the natural in his understanding. This way of thinking added to serious personal problems in Augustine's own life. Before he was a Christian, he had given himself over to many sexual perversions. In line with Greek thought, it did not matter. But after he became a Christian, he was unable to overcome those sexual behaviors until late in life. In his own writings he describes the constant battles he had, along with the related sins. This lifestyle clashed with Christian standards.

As a consequence of his failure to overcome his fleshly lusts, Augustine's view of the natural became more and more negative. In developing his theology, he took Greek thought a step further into dualism. The Greeks thought of the natural as insignificant. He concluded that it was evil.

AUGUSTINIAN THOUGHT

The Spiritual is Good   **The Natural is Evil**

Augustine began associating original sin with sexual relationships. He taught that Adam and Eve's sin somehow was related to their having sex with one another. Furthermore, he explained, all people are born in sin because they are all born as a result of a man and woman having sexual intercourse. With this way of thinking, a negative attitude was placed over the whole function of sexual relationships, even within marriage.

Origen (ca. 185-254) had similar thinking which he brought to the Church. To see the dualistic mindset he had, I can mention that he lived much of his life denying himself of natural pleasures and doing things such as sleeping on bare boards. His negative view toward sex is evident by the fact that he made himself a eunuch by crushing his own testicles with two bricks.

In history, or in modern life, when people have embraced dualistic thinking, they will follow one of two paths during their lives: licentiousness or asceticism.

Licentiousness is simply the loose, carefree living which says, "If it feels good do it." This is based on the satisfaction of all natural desires, denying morality and guilt. It is down this road that we find many of those who were raised in strict, moral, yet dualistic environments. They were unable to live up to the demands of dualism, so they eventually gave up and decided that they themselves are evil, hopelessly enslaved.

Asceticism is the other extreme where a person sees the natural world as evil, and, therefore, tries to withdraw as much as possible from the natural affairs of life. Escape, rules, laws, and stronger controls are the answers for which they must reach—none of which produce a victorious lifestyle (Col. 2:20-23).

The conclusion we can draw from history is that dualism produces bad fruit. In our society today, even in the Church, it opens the door for sexual problems to develop.

On a more personal level, we can say that an individuals with a dualistic mindset consciously and/or subconsciously see other people as divided. They tend to think the real person standing in front of them is the invisible part, while the visible, physical body is just a container. At first this may seem acceptable to many readers, but please follow with me here to learn how destructive and wrong this way of viewing others is.

When a sexually perverted man rapes a woman, he must make this division in his mind. He does not allow himself to see the victim as a person with friends, feelings, responsibilities, goals, etc. It is common for a rapist to embrace an attitude of seeing a female victim as "a slut," "a bitch," or simply as insignificant. He either must hate or be totally unfeeling toward her. Of course, he may not have this attitude before or after the violation, but during the act, he, in almost every case, must take on this dualistic frame of mind.

A man who looks at pornographic pictures similarly is divided in his thinking. He is not seeing the real people behind the images. The viewer has no thoughts or concerns about the individuals themselves. He is not experiencing sadness because of the photographed person's situation in life, nor is he concerned about that person's financial or relationship struggles. Instead, he is looking through eyes which have distanced the person away from the physical body. He sees the body as merely an object to be enjoyed.

Similarly, when a man abuses a child, he already has separated in his mind that child from real feelings, future activities, thoughts—personhood. Only as he thinks of that child as an object to be used, can he carry on with his evil behavior.

I want you to see how the soil in which sexual problems grow is very commonly dualistic thinking. Of course, I could point to sin and fleshly lusts as the root, but I am identifying the anchoring place for such lusts. The dualistic mind is a *seedbed* in which sexual problems can develop. I am not saying that dualism is the source of evil. There is a real devil, and people have lustful thoughts within themselves. However, the truth is that the person who sees others as whole people will be healthier and freer of sexual problems.

Most of the negative fruits of dualism are much

more subtle than acts of violence, rape, or sexual molestation. When children tease the homely boy at school, they are not seeing him as a person, but an object. When a husband looks condescendingly upon his overweight wife, in his mind he is separating her body from her as a person. When a male boss sexually harasses his secretary, he is denying her as a person. Racial prejudice also has at its root, dualistic thinking which separates the body from the person.

Tragically, some of the most spiritually-gifted Christians have embraced dualistic mindsets. In their endeavor to please God, they have sought a separation of themselves from the world. Teachings concerning the denial of self have captivated their consciousness. Then, when they find themselves unable to resist sin, they place stronger and stronger laws upon themselves. An entire system of thought and doctrine gradually takes over their minds. Many devoted, sincere Christians have traveled down this road and became enslaved to sexual perversions, crushed under the weight of their broken rules.

Most people enslaved to sexual sins will not get free until they retrain their minds to see others as whole people.

The man whose eyes compulsively jump from one pretty girl to another needs to tell himself that the girls he is watching are real individuals with homes, families, friends, problems, goals, feelings, etc. He will be helped by directing his attention toward their personhoods and wondering for a brief moment what responsibilities and burdens they each are carrying. For the fellow who is having difficulty in keeping his eyes off a certain woman, he may, when possible and appropriate, approach her and ask her, for example, how her day is going. As she speaks, he actually needs to listen for her to express who she is. As he tunes in to the person behind the face, he actively is healing the division in his mind and breaking dualistic thought.

The one longing to stare at pornographic pictures needs to realize that there is more to each picture than just a physical body. Real people are involved. Simply talking to other people and becoming interested in them as individuals helps the perverted mind to reform.

I do not want to make the attaining of freedom seem so easy that no effort is involved here. The Bible tells us that we do fight against a real devil (Eph. 5:12). Any person who is struggling in these areas should seek both counseling and the help of other Christians to stand with him/her. Troubled individuals may be benefited by a wide range of ministries, and they should obtain whatever help is available. However, they also must abandon dualistic ways of thinking. Healing of the dualistic mind comes with the discovery that every person upon whom one's eyes fall is a real person. The solution is not to isolate oneself from other people, but actually to engage them as people. With that revelation, a person can begin developing a biblical, whole view of people. That view, we will see more clearly in the next two chapters.

8

The Biblical View of the Physical Body

Let's now consider the proper attitude for a Christian to have toward the physical body.

When Adam and Eve were created, they were created in the image of God. The whole person—spirit, soul, and body—was created in His image. The spirit bears the image of God. The soul was created in the image of God. And the physical body is the expressed image of God in the natural realm. When God finished fashioning Adam and Eve, He declared over His work that "it was very good" (Gen. 1:31). This concept that the human body is good by God's design, and that it was created in the image of God, is the correct biblical view.

THE BIBLICAL VIEW OF MAN'S BODY

"Good"

Created in God's Image

Of course, we know that sin has corrupted humanity. Yet, we still are created in God's image. With this in mind, we need to value correctly the physical body.

Those who focus on the spiritual side of a person's nature (dualists), diminish the significance of the physical body. They tend to see it as a mere vessel or container for the soul/spirit to indwell. Dualistic Christians often quote the words of the Apostle Paul in Second Corinthians 5:1-4, where he referred to the body as an "earthly tent." They also emphasize that our physical body someday will be eliminated.

In reality the body is much more than just a tent.

In order to discover the importance of a person's body, we need to read the entire passage where Paul refers to our body as a tent.

> *For we know that if the earthly tent which is our house is torn down, we have a building from God, a house not made with hands, eternal in the heavens. For indeed in this house we groan, longing to be clothed with our dwelling from heaven; inasmuch as we, having put it on, shall not be found naked. For indeed while we are in this tent, we groan, being burdened, because we do not want to be unclothed, but to be clothed, in order that what is mortal may be swallowed up by life.* (II Cor. 5:1-4)

Paul describes how we will feel when we leave this body at death: "naked" and "unclothed." We will be *groaning and longing* to be clothed with a new body. It will be uncomfortable for us to have no body.

Our body is not just a useless container of which we hope to dispense. That is not what Paul was teaching when he called it a "tent." On the contrary, our body is a vital part of our being, and it will be difficult for us to be without it.

Furthermore, the body is an intrinsic part of our nature. In Volume II, Chapter 8, I explained how the physical body actually is involved in the daily decisions we make. I will not repeat that earlier discussion, but I can point out again that the will of man is, in part, located within the physical body. This means, above all else, that the body is not just a useless, flexible shell, but rather a part of who we are.

Next, we need to see that the physical body is *temporary* only in the sense of it someday being transformed into a new body. Paul explains in another passage (I Cor. 15:35-55) that when the final trumpet blows, our physical bodies, which have decayed in the ground, will resurrect. As the residue arises, it will be transformed into imperishable substance, and we shall receive new immortal bodies. God originally created people as three-part beings, and we will be three-part beings (including a body) for eternity.

This concept has escaped many Christians. They wrongly envision a *bodiless eternity*. They think they will be floating around on clouds, with a smile on their face, in a mystical, spiritual state forever. That idea is foreign to the Bible.

The idea of a *disembodied eternity* came from the influence of Greek thought. Remember how the Greek philosophers separated the spiritual world from the natural, and then thought negatively about the natural? Those who embraced that way of thinking looked forward to a day when they could escape this world and leave their physical bodies behind. That was the Greek concept of the afterlife, before Christianity was brought to that society. None of our early Christian writings (from the First Century) teach a disembodied eternity. That way of thinking gradually developed in the Church during the Third and Fourth Centuries, as Greek philosophy began influencing the Church. As a result, the established Church at that time embraced the disembodied view of eternity, and many Christians even today still have a mental picture of heaven as a place in the clouds for smiling, ghost-like people.

What the Bible teaches is quite different. God will create a new heaven and new Earth (Rev. 20:11-21:1; I Peter 3:10-13). We will not be floating in the clouds. In fact, we will not even be living in the new heaven, but rather on the new Earth—with two feet on the ground. Read about it in your Bible (Rev. 21)! All believers in Jesus will receive new, immortal bodies. They then will be walking around on a literal Earth. We will exist for eternity as three-part beings with an imperishable body.

To see this more clearly, we can look at the nature of our Lord Jesus. "And the Word became flesh..." (John 1:14). He did not come to Earth and *dwell in* flesh. No. The Word *became* flesh. He took on human nature.

After Jesus died on the cross, He arose on the third day. He came forth in His body. That body was transformed and glorified. It was not discarded, but changed. The grave in which He was placed is empty today. The substance of His body was used.

Today, Jesus is sitting in heaven on a throne at the right hand of the Father. Someday He will return to Earth. When we get to see Him, we will look at a real face and a real body. He did not take on a body for just a short period of time. The Word became flesh and He has chosen to dwell among us forever. He is not in some mystical, spiritual form, but like unto people, yet glorified.

When the apostles first saw Jesus after His resurrection, they made the mistake of thinking that He was "a spirit." Luke reported:

> *But they were startled and frightened and thought that they were seeing a spirit.* (Luke 24:37)

Jesus corrected their thinking and reassured them, saying:

> *"See My hands and My feet, that it is I Myself; touch Me and see, for a spirit does not have flesh and bones as you see that I have."* (Luke 24:39)

Notice that Jesus specifically denied the thinking that

He was "a spirit." Today Jesus has hands and feet. Of course, His body has been transformed into a spiritual state, but it is important to note that He still has a body, a soul, and a spirit.

Look carefully at the transformation that Jesus experienced after His resurrection. The corruptible body He had while on Earth was transformed into an incorruptible one. Paul explained in First Corinthians 15:34-58 that after death, the perishable body is changed into an imperishable body (15:42). This transformation someday will happen to all believers in Christ (I Cor. 15:51-54), but here it is important to note that Jesus already went through that process. He was the "first-born" of many brethren. As such, He has a body made not of corruptible material from Earth, but of incorruptible substance from heaven.

In regard to this transformation, the Apostle Paul made an interesting comparison between Adam and Jesus. He wrote:

> *So also is the resurrection of the dead. It is sown a perishable body, it is raised an imperishable body; it is sown in dishonor, it is raised in glory; it is sown in weakness, it is raised in power; it is sown a natural body, it is raised a spiritual body. If there is a natural body, there is also a spiritual body. So also it is written, "The first man, Adam, became a living soul." The last*

Adam became a life-giving spirit.
(I Cor. 15:42-45)

Notice that the words "spiritual" and "natural" are being contrasted throughout these verses. In referring to Jesus as a life-giving spirit, Paul is not calling Jesus "a spirit." Rather, Paul was explaining that Jesus has a "spiritual body"—a body that is made of immortal, heavenly material. As Adam's body was formed from the dust of the Earth, Jesus' new body was formed from the substance of heaven. Here we see the use of the word spirit to mean spiritual in nature. The main point of the text is that Jesus still has a body; that body, however, has been transformed from its natural existence into a spiritual state.

The Apostle Paul wrote these words in First Corinthians in order to encourage the Christians and let them know that they too would someday receive spiritual bodies.

> *...in a moment, in the twinkling of an eye, at the last trumpet; for the trumpet will sound, and the dead will be raised imperishable, and we shall be changed. For this perishable must put on the imperishable, and this mortal must put on immortality.* (I Cor. 15:52-53)

On that transformation day, we still will be three-part beings, but our resurrected bodies will take on a spiritual nature.

Our Future State

Spirit   Soul   Glorified
Body

After the final judgment, those whose names are written in the Lamb's book of life will live on the new Earth (Rev. 21). They will have real bodies which are not subject to disease or pain, but incorruptible. We will not spend eternity in suspended animation just praising God. We will have definite positions and responsibilities throughout eternity. We will have jobs and real tasks to accomplish. There will not be any curse upon the new Earth, but we will be active and our labors will flourish. We do not know all that is in store for us, but we do know that the future will be glorious.

This biblical view of eternity helps people hold a proper view of their bodies today. The dualistic, or Greek view, is wrong. Seeing that our bodies will play a role in our eternal existence elevates our understanding of their role in our present existence.

We were created as three-part beings and we will have three parts for eternity. Now while we are alive on Earth, we must accept our bodies as a part of our beings. It is, in fact, a beautiful part of Creation. It is the means by which we can live and accomplish God's will in this natural world. The natural realm itself is good, as God declared it to be. We live here. We have three wonderful parts to our nature. We must live as whole human beings. We must think of ourselves as whole individuals.

9

Embrace Your Life on the Earth

The people most prone to dualistic ways of thinking are those living in difficult circumstances who would enjoy thoughts of escaping this natural realm. At the root of dualism is a negative view of the world, life, and self.

It is enlightening to know the circumstances surrounding some of the major proponents of dualism such as Augustine and Watchman Nee. Until late in life Augustine was unable to conquer his sexual passions, and he lived in disgust of his own physical existence. Watchman Nee also lived under tremendous physical stress. In fact, he completed his best-known book, *The Spiritual Man* (sometimes published in three volumes), at the age of 25, while suffering with tuberculosis on what was thought to be his deathbed. Although he recovered over time, he continued under heavy persecution during most of his life.

There are many people who have lived in difficult circumstances physically, emotionally, or spiritually. They are the ones most prone to interpret life and the Bible with a perspective of rejection pertaining to the natural things. They seek refuge in the spiritual realm. There is, of course, benefit in finding refuge in God, but the negative basis for such a pursuit leads to subtle deceptions.

A Bible verse often misunderstood by dualists is John 12:25, where Jesus said:

> *"He who loves his life loses it; and*
> *he who hates his life in this world*
> *shall keep it to life eternal."*

The dualist may take this verse and teach that we actually and literally should hate being alive. The Greek word for life in the first part of this verse is *psuche*, and, therefore, the dualist further can justify his/her rejection of his/her natural existence, by saying we are not to love our *psuche life*, that is our *soul life*.

In actuality, this verse is not teaching what filters through the dualist's eyes. The same exhortation from our Lord can be found in the other three gospels, as well. In Matthew 16:25, Mark 8:35, and Luke 9:24, the same exhortations to hate one's soul life are followed by these words:

> *"For what will a man be profited,*
> *if he gains the whole world, and*
> *forfeits his soul? Or what will a*
> *man give in exchange for his*
> *soul?"*   (Matt. 16:26)
> [Mark 8:36-37 and Luke 9:25
> read similarly.]

Notice that this verse gives us a contextual understanding of how we are to look at our soul. The truth is that our soul is the most valuable thing we possess. What could we ever give in exchange for it? The obvious answer is, "nothing."

This conclusion is exactly the opposite of that at which the dualist arrives. After isolating John 12:25 from its context, the dualist concludes that we should hate our souls. In actuality, it is our souls that we are told to treasure above all else.

What does it mean, then, to "hate our life in this world"? The emphasis is on the phrase, "in this world." We are to hate the thought of losing our soul in this world.

To confirm this, consider our Lord's words in Matthew 6:24.

> *"No one can serve two masters; for either he will hate the one and love the other, or he will hold to one and despise the other. You cannot serve God and mammon."*
> (Matt. 6:24)

According to this verse, every human being will give his/her life to God or to mammon. It is in this sense that we lose our soul life.

Christians are not supposed to hate their lives. Nor do we hate this world. What we must hate is *the losing of our soul to this world*. That thought should be despicable to us. Our souls are the most treasured things we have. We must love our souls and loose them, that is, place them, in the care of God.

This understanding is completely different from

the dualists'. They want to justify their hate, both for this world and for their own lives. This attitude is wrong.

Much of the confusion about hating this world stems from differing uses of the term *world*. The Bible uses this term in at least three different ways. In John 3:16 we are told, "For God so loved the world...." Here we understand that the word *world* refers to the people who live on the Earth. In other passages it refers to the natural creation—the mountains, trees, oceans, and everything we can see around us (i.e., Acts 17:24). This natural world has been affected negatively by the sin of humanity, but it is good in its original design. A third definition focuses upon the evil system over which Satan rules. The Bible tells us that Satan is the ruler of this world (John 14:30); as such, the world is our enemy (John 15:19; I Cor. 2:12). Since all three of these definitions of the term *world* are used in the Bible, we must be careful how we use these terms as we communicate with each other.

As Christians, we should love the world as God does when speaking of the people who inhabit the Earth. We also should love the natural world because of the beauty in which it was created. However, we must not love the world of Satan's domain and his work here (I John 2:15-16; James 4:4).

With this understanding, we can embrace the proper view of our life here on this planet. Dualists tend to hate their existence within this natural world, and that is wrong. Not only is it wrong, but it causes the dualist to waste much of the lifetime he/she has been given here. Allow me to explain.

Dualists consciously or subconsciously think of the world (the general population) around them as evil, so they ultimately try to live in isolation. Rather than being a light to the world, they withdraw and never influence, in any significant way, anyone outside their small circle of Christian friends.

Dualists who do get involved with efforts to change society are ineffective for several reasons. The attitude of isolationism tends to breed an evil suspicion toward others. As a consequence, they keep themselves aloof and rarely are able to develop the working relationships with people that are necessary to accomplish significant change. They set out from the perspective, "It's us versus them; the good guys against the bad guys." At the very start, they believe in their hearts that everyone is against them, and, therefore, they make enemies and create unnecessary resistance. Even evangelism is difficult, because when Christians have judgments within their hearts against the people to whom they are talking, the listeners can sense it and they respond negatively.

In addition, the statement, "you cannot change what you hate," proves true again and again in the life of the dualist. Members of dualistic groups, whether or not they realize it, tend to breed a hatred toward society and anything which does not conform to their ideals. It is common to hear sarcastic remarks being passed around such groups pertaining to the evils of our government, how our educational system is totally corrupt, etc. These statements may have some truth in them, but attitudes of hate toward others, not wanting to be involved, or thinking that the problems are too big to change, are contrary to the nature of God and His commission to believers.

When a group of Christians develops dualistic concepts, it tends to draw within itself and become very ingrown and stagnant. Its members may form into some type of separatist community or they may remain living in society but have their defenses so hardened against outsiders that no one from outside their own group can enter.

There are many positive aspects to the bonding together of Christians in a community fashion; however, the dualistic mentality too easily leads to a pride in which those involved start to think of themselves as more holy than outsiders. It is common for dualists to talk about the "select few," "the true believers," or "the remnant." Deception commonly creeps into such groups, and in time they experience terrible destruction.

Another problem which dualism promotes is legalism. Because the natural world is viewed as evil, there typically develops a "do not touch, do not taste" attitude, against which we are warned in the Bible (Col. 2:21-23). For example, the proper Christian view toward food is that "...everything created by God is good..." (I Tim. 4:4). In contrast, dualists often exalt fasting and denounce the enjoyment of food in an unbiblical fashion. Similarly, the pleasures within marriage are sometimes looked down upon as unholy.

In addition, such things as newspapers, sports activities, radio, medicine, and technological advancements sometimes are condemned categorically. Of course, every Christian should exercise wisdom with regard to his/her involvements, but it is legalism in these areas about which I am warning. The mindset of viewing everything that is natural as less than God's best, develops into an endless number of rules and regulations which keep a person from enjoying what God has created for us.

We also see Christians who embrace dualistic ideas becoming unable to function successfully in this natural world. Because they consciously or subconsciously think of the natural things as evil, they have less and less energy to do what needs to be done. The importance of working at a job diminishes. Fixing the house or the car may be viewed as unnecessary and too temporal. Caring for one's own appearance and physical body can seem vain. Dualistic individuals often find themselves losing interest in accomplishing anything in this natural world. As a consequence of not putting time and energy into that which needs their attention, they gradually slip into poverty, physical ailments, and marriage problems. Dualists commonly have difficulties in one or more of these areas.

When individuals hate this world in their heart, they emanate spiritual energy which forbids them full access to it. Dualists do not consider their possessions as gifts from God, but rather as "junk" or just "stuff weighing them down." Subconsciously they may have judgments against people who are financially blessed, thinking of them as being less pleasing to God than those who are poor. Work is viewed not as a privilege, but a necessary evil. This leads to frustration because dualists try desperately to live according to what they believe, but it simply does not produce victory nor abundance. People can neither receive nor enjoy the blessings of God if they are rejecting those very things in their hearts.

In addition, dualists find relationships with people hindered. I already mentioned the suspicion that is bred toward outsiders, but even those who should be "insiders" suffer. Because the dualists' hearts are directed toward the spiritual side, they cannot give themselves fully to their spouses in marriage relationships. Children may grow up unable ever fully to touch the heart of a dualistic parent. Because that parent is detached and uninvolved, the children very often begin rebelling against anything associated with the Church. Bonding is almost impossible, because the dualist constructs an invisible wall within his/her heart toward natural attachments.

In today's world, there are some Christians who develop attitudes about faith that lead to dualistic lifestyles. Some confuse faith with denial of reality and eventually detach from the natural world. James explained in the Bible that faith which does not produce works is dead (James 2:14-26). True faith leads people to face their problems with confidence, rather than deny them.

Although I am pointing out all of these negative tendencies in dualistic Christians, I also acknowledge a seriousness and earnestness often seen in their walks with God. Because they separate themselves from society, responsibilities, and the concerns of the world, they frequently appear very intense and committed to God. Indeed, many of them dedicate more time to prayer and worship because their interests are not divided among people and natural concerns. I have met several Christian leaders whom I have greatly admired, in spite of the fact that they had dualistic tendencies. Having said that, I believe that we all can be zealous in our walks with God, while at the same time holding to a healthier form of Christianity.

To develop a proper Bible-based perspective, we must perceive of the natural realm not as evil, but as redeemable. We must lose our lives to God, which means that we will do His will in the Earth. Our gifts and abilities are the means by which we are to "work out" in this natural world that which God has given us to do. The natural world is not something from which we must escape, but rather the realm in which we are to demonstrate and establish the kingdom of God.

Simply put, Earth is where we live.

And it is not a bad place to live! After God finished each of His creative acts, He declared, "It is good." Yes, sin has had its effect upon this world, but nature is still abundant and glorious (I Cor. 15:40-41).

Even life itself is something to be enjoyed. Solomon, the man endowed with wisdom from God, wrote:

> *There is nothing better for a man than to eat and drink and tell himself that his labor is good. This also I have seen, that it is from the hand of God.* (Eccl. 2:24)

This is the attitude Christians should have concerning

their time upon the Earth. Life is a gift. The ongoing daily Christian life should be one of rejoicing and thankfulness.

Christians should embrace their lives upon the Earth, that is, accept who God created them to be and fulfill the role He has given them. Only if they understand that they were created to live successfully in this world will they, indeed, live successfully. If they reject their physical side, they will view this life as only a burden from which to escape. It is not that bad!

People who think that their natural life is evil will have a difficult time experiencing the beauty of a mountain, the colors of a flower, the laughter of a child, the love of a spouse, or the blessings with which God is trying to surround them. When these principles are explained clearly to people who have been dualistic, they begin enjoying more fully the simple pleasures, such as eating a good meal and spending time relaxing with others. Strict dualists rarely allow themselves to experience these joys. Mild dualists enjoy these things from time to time, but feel a little guilty about it. You need not be among either group. God wants you to be happy.

10

You Are a Human Being

Dualism is a lie in people's minds and hearts that can usher them into blindness and slavery. I have discussed the resulting bondages related to sexual perversions, legalism, defeated lifestyles, isolationism, poverty, broken relationships, and false spiritual influences. Here I want to deal a final death blow to dualism and declare a truth that will set people free.

I am offering you a more biblical view of how people were created, and, therefore, how we must function in this world. I want to answer the basic question, "What is a human being?"

The easiest way to answer this is to challenge one more dualistic deception. This one pertains to another false doctrine which dualists sometimes develop from a mistranslation of John 4:24. This verse records a statement made by Jesus, one which has been translated from the original language differently in different Bible translations. The King James Version of this verse says:

> *"God is a Spirit: and they that worship him must worship him in spirit and in truth."*

Dualists like to use this translation and emphasize how God is said to be "a spirit." From this point the dualists' argument is as follows:

1. God is a spirit;
2. Man was created in the image of God;
3. Therefore, man is *a spirit*.

The last point here is presented as a logically deduced conclusion. The teaching goes on to suggest that people were created by God as "spirit-beings." This doctrine has been taught in many Christian circles, and the conclusion that a human being is *a spirit* has profound implications, most of which are wrong.

Of course, people need to be taught about the spiritual side to their existence. People today are often so materially and naturally conscious that they ignore the role that the spirit within them plays. However, to call a person *a spirit-being* is biblically wrong. Please let me show this to you.

Look carefully at the three points made in the argument above. The first statement, "God is a spirit," is not in the Bible. The King James Version of John 4:24 words it this way, but in the original Greek, in which the New Testament was written, there are no indefinite articles. This means that the letter "a", preceding the word *spirit* was added by the Bible translators of the King James Version. If you have a King James Bible, you will be helped in your understanding if you cross out the indefinite article and read our Lord's words as, "God is spirit." This is how most other Bible translations read, giving us a truer interpretation of the original meaning.*

This change may seem insignificant to you at first, but the fact that God is *spirit*, rather than *a spirit*, changes much in our understanding.

The word *spirit* is translated from the Greek word *pneuma,* and it can be used in several different ways. For example, *pneuma* can refer to *the spirit part of a person*, or to *the Holy Spirit*, or to *the breath*, or to *the nature of the spiritual world*.

It is this last meaning that we see being used in the context of John 4:24. In that passage, Jesus was discussing with a Samaritan woman about worshiping God. The woman was asking the Lord on which mountain people should worship (John 4:20). She was focused on natural forms of worship and was asking "where" people should worship. In answer to that question, Jesus pointed out that God did not care where a person worshiped because He is not physical in nature. God is spirit, meaning He exists in the spiritual dimension.

The Bible clearly tells us in other passages that God is not just "a spirit." In several verses we are told

---

* The seriousness of this error can be seen more clearly if I point out a similar error made by the translators of the *New World Translation*, which is the official Bible of the Jehovah Witnesses. In John 1:1 they added the indefinite article "a" before the word, "God." As a consequence, they teach that Jesus was "a god," rather than God. I point this out to show you how the insertion of one letter, "a," can lead to tremendous error. Although we may not like to admit to such an error in a Bible translation such as the *King James Version*, which has been so widely used by Christians, it is true and it should be recognized.

that God has both a soul and a spirit. Both the soul
and the spirit are spiritual in nature because we can
neither see nor physically touch them, but we must
know that *there is more to God than just a spirit.*

To confirm this, read God's own words as recorded
in Hebrews 10:38, concerning His own soul.

> *But My righteous one shall live*
> *   by faith;*
> *And if he shrinks back, My soul*
> *   has no pleasure in him.*

God states here that He has a soul in addition to a
spirit.

In the Old Testament we see similar declarations.
For example, when God was speaking about releasing
blessings on His people, He said:

> *"Moreover, I will make My dwel-*
> *ling among you, and My soul will*
> *not reject you."*   (Lev. 26:11)

Using the same reference to His own soul, God spoke
about the curses He would release.

> *"...My soul shall abhor you."*
>   (Lev. 26:30)

In First Samuel 2:35, we read God's words:

> *"But I will raise up for Myself a*
> *faithful priest who will do accord-*

> *ing to what is in My heart and in*
> *My soul...."*

Throughout the Bible, God Himself speaks about His own soul.

Note in the above verses that God speaks of *His soul as the core of His own being*, from which He makes decisions of acceptance or rejection.*

Consider what this implies when we talk about a person being created in the image of God. God is not "a spirit." Therefore, man is not "a spirit," nor is he "a spirit-being." If a person is created in the image of God, then he/she consists of at least a soul and a spirit. More than that, his/her entire being is created in the image of God. The body was designed by the same Maker as the spirit/soul. The body is simply the natural expression of a person's invisible existence. We are created in God's image—spirit/soul/body.

Furthermore, the soul (not the spirit) plays the predominant role within our being.

This is in agreement with the rest of the Bible. *Nowhere in the Bible are people called spirits or spirit-beings.* In fact, we are told specifically that Adam was created a "living soul" (Gen. 2:7). When the Bible speaks of individuals referring to one part of their being, their souls are the focal point. For example, in Acts 2:41 we are told that 3,000 souls were added to the Church on Pentecost Day. In the Bible people are

---

* I believe in the Trinity, but here I simply am trying to give biblical evidence for the existence of God's soul and spirit. In another book, entitled, *Who Is God,* I have discussed more clearly the nature of God.

pictured not as spirits but as three-part beings, with their souls playing the predominant role.

Why am I making such a point of this? Because the doctrine which views a person as "a spirit" or a "spirit-being" only adds to the dualist's deceptions. The Christian who truly believes that he/she is a spirit, rather than a whole person, ends up denying a part of his/her own nature. If a person thinks he/she is a spirit-being, he/she is going to try to live as a spirit-being. This is dualism at its worst!

Let's contrast the nature of humanity with the nature of true spirit-beings. Demons, for example, do not have a physical body. They exist in the spirit realm. In order to influence this natural world, they seek a human vessel through whom to work. We are shown in the Bible that they even try to inhabit human beings. It is in this sense that they are different from us. They are, indeed, spirit-beings, created different from human beings.

Consider again the words exchanged when the disciples first saw Jesus after His resurrection. They "thought that they were seeing a spirit" (Luke 24:37). Jesus corrected their thinking, saying, "See My hands and My feet, that it is I Myself; touch Me and see, for a spirit does not have flesh and bones as you see that I have" (Luke 24:39). Jesus took on our nature, hence, He is not a spirit. Although His body is now glorified, He took on a three-part nature, the same as you and I have.

This may seem very simplistic to you, but let me state it as clearly as I can: *You are not a spirit-being; you are a human being*.

I am not trying to lower in your mind the grandeur in which God created people. Unlike the animals, we were created in the very image of God. Furthermore, as Christians, we are human beings in whom God dwells. We are partakers of divine nature. The life of God flows through us. However, we have three parts to our nature. We are human. This is the biblical view.

This leaves the dualist with one remaining question: Where should the ultimate authority be in the Christian's life? Dualists, in over-emphasizing the spirit of a person, sometimes will summarize their doctrines by saying that every person is a spirit-being, and that a person's nature should be arranged in a hierarchy, with the spirit as the master, the soul as the servant, and the body as the slave.

DUALISTIC HIERARCHY

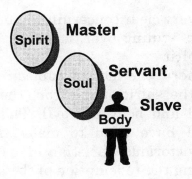

Is this true?

No. The Bible does not give us any hierarchy concerning our three-part nature. Furthermore, many

Scriptures contradict the dualist's doctrine of ultimate authority in the spirit of a person.

For example, First Corinthians 14:32 tells us that "the spirits of prophets are subject to prophets." You cannot "subject the spirit" and at the same time have it as the ultimate authority in your being.

Furthermore, Proverbs tells us:

> *He who is slow to anger is better*
> *than the mighty,*
> *And he who rules his spirit, than*
> *he who captures a city.*
> (Prov. 16:32)

> *Like a city that is broken into and*
> *without walls*
> *Is a man who has no control over*
> *his spirit.* (Prov. 25:28)

The Bible is very clear concerning a person—including the Christian—ruling over, controlling, and subjecting his/her spirit.

Furthermore, the idea of subjecting the soul and the body to the spirit stems from the dualistic view that the soul and body are evil. That contradicts a main point I have tried to make throughout this volume: the victorious Christian life is one of redemption—including the redemption of the soul and body.

To ask the question, "What should be the final authority in a person's being?" is to misunderstand how God created us. The will of a person is not limited to just the spirit, just the soul, nor just the human body. In Volume II, Chapter 4, I explained how the will of a person permeates his/her entire being—spirit, soul, and body.

Hence, the Christian life is not meant to be one of denying, rejecting, or subjecting one part over the others. Paul prayed that we may be sanctified throughout our beings—spirits, souls, and bodies (I Thess. 5:23). As we are sanctified, our spirits become one with God's Spirit; the desires of our souls come into alignment with God's desires; and the desires of our bodies conform to His will. Our entire beings then come into conformity to God's will.

We are not to have one part of our beings fighting nor dominating any other part. Rather, we are to be filled with the Holy Spirit throughout our beings so that everything within us is in harmony and submission to God.

A CHRISTIAN SANCTIFIED BODY, SOUL, AND SPIRIT

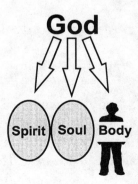

Recognizing this truth, I still can point out the central role of a person's soul. Genesis 2:7 tells us that

God breathed into the body of Adam, and "man became a living soul." That is what man is! The soul is
the focal point of a person's being; however, all of a
person's being is to be alive and responsive to God.

Conclusion

In this volume I have attempted to lay out a biblically-accurate view of our nature and how we relate to both the natural and spiritual worlds. In doing this, I have challenged and uprooted some misconceptions to which many Christians in the past have held . I trust that you have been able to see the significance of these, and, hence, escape any dualistic tendencies within your own life

Still there is a warning that I must include before closing this volume. I have explained how a dualistic lifestyle leads to several deceptions and serious problems, however, in an attempt to escape dualism some may go to the other extreme and misjudge Christians who are in some unique situations of life. Please allow me to explain.

Consider Mary and Martha, two sisters about whom we read in Luke 10:38-42. In that passage, we see Mary sitting at the feet of Jesus and attentively listening to His words. At the same time, Martha was busy working to make arrangements for her guests. In the midst of this situation, Martha became frustrated with her inactive sister Mary, and she complained to Jesus. If we were to analyze Mary and Martha in light of dualism, we would note that Mary was detached from the natural world and acting irresponsibly. Yet Jesus commends Mary and corrects Martha for being so worried about natural affairs (Luke 10:41-42).

What are we supposed to do with this? Abandon our own responsibilities and go sit at the feet of Jesus for the rest of our days? Well, it is true that Mary had chosen that which pleased our Lord at that time. However, Mary was not embracing a dualistic lifestyle, but rather taking a moment to sit at our Lord's feet, as we all should do.

As Mary at the feet of Jesus, there should be many times in the lives of Christians when they are captivated with the presence of God. We can compare it with two young people falling in love. Young lovers may at times appear "out of touch" with the world around them. Sometimes they seem irresponsible in their natural affairs. However, the experience of falling in love is a precious, holy time of life. In the same way, it is healthy and normal for children of God to have periods in their lives when they are so enthralled with the Person of God that everything else fades in importance. This is not to condone dualism, but to recognize moments in our lives when we become captivated spiritually. These times always must be followed by a return to living out our Christianity in this natural world.

Not only should we talk about a love relationship with our God, but there also may be times when a Christian simply is caught up in the Spirit. To the onlooker, that may appear as if he/she is being dualistic, for, indeed, the believer in such a state may lose touch with natural reality for a time and focus completely on the Spirit. An example of this would be the Apostle John when he received the visions which he recorded in the book of Revelation. He wrote that he was "in the Spirit on the Lord's day" (Rev. 1:10). In that condition John was not thinking about his financial concerns nor the people around him. In fact, he probably was detached completely from thoughts of this natural world. However, when he wrote "on the Lord's day," it is evident that he was not in that condition 24 hours a day, nor every day. Hence, we must conclude that he was not promoting a dualistic lifestyle but describing an experience he had with God.

Finally, I want to mention the times of being focused completely on spiritual things need not be brief. God may take a Christian into a season of his/her life when he/she is consumed with intercession and prayer for a longer period. God also may take a person through a time of refashioning his/her character requiring deep spiritual renewal. Such a period may last days, weeks, or longer. In saying this, I am not re-opening the door for a dualistic lifestyle, but rather acknowledging workings of God which may temporarily separate us from natural concerns.

Having made these statements, we are now ready to go on. In this volume I have attempted to impact upon your mind the fact that you are a human being. As a human, you have the residue of God's breath within you. Being a Christian means you also have the fresh breath of the Holy Spirit in you. These facts will enable you to live in this natural world, supernaturally. How this is done, I will continue discussing in the volumes which follow.

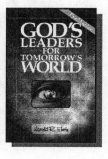

PRECIOUS IN HIS SIGHT A Fresh Look at the Nature of Man
During the Fourth Century Augustine taught about the nature of
man using as his key Scripture a verse in the book of Romans which
had been mistranslated. Since that time the Church has embraced
a false concept of man which has negatively influenced every area
of Christianity. It is time for Christians to come out of darkness!
This book, considered by many to be Harold Eberle's greatest
work, has implications upon our understanding of sin, salvation,
Who God is, evangelism, the world around us and how we can live
the daily, victorious lifestyle.

YOU SHALL RECEIVE POWER

Moving Beyond Pentecostal & Charismatic Theology
God's Spirit will fill you in measures beyond what you are
experiencing presently. This is not just about Pentecostal or
Charismatic blessings. There is something greater. It is for all
Christians, and it will build a bridge between those Christians
who speak in tongues and those who do not. It is time for the
whole Church to take a fresh look at the work of the Holy Spirit
in our individual lives. This book will help you. It will challenge
you, broaden your perspective, set you rejoicing, fill you with
hope, and leave you longing for more of God.

DEAR PASTORS AND TRAVELING MINISTERS,

Here is a manual to help pastors and traveling ministers relate and
minister together effectively. Topics are addressed such as ethical
concerns, finances, authority, scheduling,..... In addition to deal-
ing with real-life situations, an appendix is included with very
practical worksheets to offer traveling ministers and local pastors
a means to communicate with each other. Pastors and traveling
ministers can make their lives and work much easier by using this
simple, yet enlightening, manual.

DEVELOPING A PROSPEROUS SOUL
VOL I: HOW TO OVERCOME A POVERTY MIND-SET
VOL II: HOW TO MOVE INTO GOD'S
FINANCIAL BLESSINGS

There are fundamental changes you can
make in the way you think which will help
release God's blessings. This is a balanced
look at the promises of God with practical
steps you can take to move into financial
freedom. It is time for Christians to recap-
ture the financial arena.

GRACE...THE POWER TO REIGN

The Light Shining from Romans 5-8

We struggle against sin and yearn for God's highest. Yet, on a bad day it is as as if we are fighting with gravity. Questions go unanswered:

- Where is the power to overcome temptations and trials?
- Is God really willing to breathe into us so that these dry bones can live and we may stand strong?

For anyone who ever has clenched his fist in the struggle to live godly, here are the answers. Just as there is a force in the world pushing us to sin, there is a greater force flowing from God which can lift us, transform us, and make us what He wants us to be. It is grace! It is grace which few have grasped, yet, so many have sought desperately. Now you can find it.

BRINGING THE FUTURE INTO FOCUS

An Introduction to the Progressive Christian Worldview

What does the future hold? Will there be peace or war? Are the people of God going to rise up in glory and unity or will they be overcome by apathy and deception? Is Jesus coming for a spotless Bride or is He going to rescue a tattered band of zealots out of a wicked chaotic mess? Where is God taking humanity in the Twenty-First Century?

This book will answer your questions and fill you with hope.

IF GOD IS GOOD,
WHY IS THERE SO MUCH SUFFERING AND PAIN?

Life isn't fair! Terrorist bombings. Ethnic cleansing. Body-ravaging diseases. Murder. Child abuse. Natural disasters. Genetic maladies. These travesties, global and seemingly relentless, drive us to the limits of our reasoning. When pain and suffering invade our well-laid plans for a good life, we ask the gut question: Why, God, why? In this book, Harold R. Eberle evaluates the role God plays in the Earth, explores the origin of suffering, and reassures us of God kind intentions toward us.

WORLDCAST MINISTRIES

A significant portion of the profit from book sales goes to the support of interdenominational Christian missions, Bible colleges, charitable work, and orphanages in developing countries around the world. This work is done through the oversight of Worldcast Ministries, which is an organization overseen by Harold R. Eberle and a staff of volunteer and paid workers. Worldcast Ministries is a ministry based on the belief that God is raising the Church up to a position of unity, maturity, and glory. We believe that the greatest revival the world has ever seen will take place between now and the Second Coming of our Lord Jesus Christ.

If you are looking for something meaningful in which to be involved, we welcome your financial support and we encourage you to join us in helping fulfill the Great Commission to go and make disciples of all nations.

To place an order or to check current prices call:
1-800-308-5837 within the USA or:
509-248-5837 from outside the USA
(MasterCard/Visa accepted)

Worldcast Publishing
P.O. Box 10653
Yakima, WA 98909-1653

E-mail: office@worldcastpublishing.com
Web Site: www.worldcastpublishing.com
Some books available as an audiobook on cassette tapes.